Pacem in Terris

a love story

Pacem in Terris
a love story

by

Frederick Franck
a love story is a life story

Drawings and Sculpture by
FREDERICK FRANCK

Photographs by John Lewis Stage

CODHILL PRESS • NEW PALTZ

ALSO BY FREDERICK FRANCK

Open Wide Please
1956
*Days With Albert Schweitzer
1959
*My Friend in Africa
1960
African Sketchbook
1961
My Eye Is in Love
1963
Outsider in the Vatican
1965
I Love Life
1967
Exploding Church
1968
Simenon's Paris
1970
*The Zen of Seeing
1973
Pilgrimage to Now/Here
1973
An Encounter with Oomoto
1975
*Zen and Zen Classics,
Selections From R.H. Blyth, ed.
1977
Every One, The Timeless Myth
of Everyman Reborn
1978

The Awakened Eye
1979
*Art As a Way
1981
*The Supreme Koan
1982
*The Buddha Eye:
An Anthology of the Kyoto School, ed.
1982
Echoes from the Bottomless Well
1985
*Life Drawing Life
1989
*A Little Compendium on That Which Matters
1989
*To Be Human Against All Odds
1991
*Zen Seeing, Zen Drawing: Meditation in Action
1993
*Fingers Pointing Toward the Sacred
1994
*The Tao of the Cross & The Oxherding Parable
1996
*What Does It Mean to be Human?
1998
*Beyond Hiroshima
1999
*The Angelic Verses
1999

* All the books marked with an asterisk are available at the gallery at Pacem in Terris or from your bookstore

Library of Congress Cataloging-in-Publication Data

Franck, Frederick, 1909 -
Pacem in Terris: a love story / Frederick Franck; drawings and sculpture by Frederick Franck.
p.cm.
ISBN 1-930337-02-7 (alk. paper)
1.Franck, Frederick, 1909- 2. Artists--United States--Biography. 3.Pacem in Terris
(Warwick, N.Y.)--History. I.Title.

N6537.F727A2 2000
709'.2--dc21
[B]   00-025446

Frontispiece: *The door: a large wooden sculpture, the Sun, with a glass jewel as its center. It turns around a spindle, so that only one person can enter at a time, without talking, alone, as one enters and exits life*

for Claske and
my son Lukas

Contents

Chapter One	9
Chapter Two	23
Chapter Three	29
Chapter Four	35
Chapter Five	39
Chapter Six	49
Chapter Seven	53
Chapter Eight	57
Chapter Nine	63
Chapter Ten	69
Chapter Eleven	79
Chapter Twelve	89
Chapter Thirteen	99
Coda	117
Appendix	119

Old Man of the River

This book is really its (Pacem in Terris) *story: the story of a garbage dump transformed into a sanctuary, for once, instead of the other way around.*

ONE

Two months ago I gave a lecture at a New Jersey college about my latest book, *What Does It Mean to Be Human?* As my wife and I exited from the driveway, our car was hit, full force, by a van ignoring the traffic light. We survived with fractured legs and ribs, in a kind of limbo between CAT scans, sonograms, blood transfusions, and X-rays, immobile in plaster casts.

On our way home from the hospital weeks later, I stopped the ambulance in front of Pacem in Terris. So it did exist! Pacem was not a drug-induced *fata morgana!* This book is really its story: the story of a garbage dump transformed into a sanctuary, for once, instead of the other way around. It can be read as such, or as an artist's ego trip, but I have turned ninety, when ego trips have become quaintly obsolete. After our collision, just being alive revealed itself to be a sheer bonus – still being alive together, however brief the reprieve, sheer grace.

The day before the accident, I had been working on an updated edition of our little visitor's guide, "The Story of Pacem in Terris," "Peace on Earth," the transreligious sanctuary that for the past thirty-five years has been our poor man's folly, and our *raison d'être.* I found the photographs I had gathered for it under the pyramid of six weeks' accumulated papers on my desk. They dated back to 1962 when Pacem was still a garbage

Above: Rising from the earth, sinking back into it. I finished and placed it the day before the accident! March 25, 1999
Left: First glances at the dump that was to become a sanctuary

dump camouflaged by a thick quilt of weeds in summer. A second photo showed it as a large hole on the roadside across the Wawayanda River, depository of car transmissions, dented refrigerators, tree trunks, dirty mattresses. There was also a snapshot of the ruin seen in the autumn when the leaves had fallen and the fieldstone walls that enclosed the dump had become visible. But the revelatory one was the close-up of one of the window holes after some of the junk had been removed. It proved by its structure that what we had purchased for eight hundred dollars – merely for protection against "developers" – was much more than a garbage dump. It was a unique treasure, a priceless heirloom under its disguise of filth.

I had wondered, while digging out the debris, why that ruin at times filled me with an almost overwhelming awe, as if every stone that became visible once the rubble was removed revealed itself as a precious relic. The close-up of the empty window hole showed clearly, dramatically, how indeed each single block of fieldstone had been shaped, not by some machinery, but by a human hand holding chisel and hammer, trimming, furrowing, smoothing each side to fit its neighbors with such precision that these hundreds of building blocks could form the

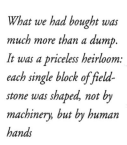

What we had bought was much more than a dump. It was a priceless heirloom: each single block of fieldstone was shaped, not by machinery, but by human hands

massive walls without any mortar to hold them together. The walls still stand intact after braving two hundred years of storms, floods, frost, and fires.

The old mill had been built in the late eighteenth century, around the time of the Declaration of Independence. It was in its way still "pre-American," in a sense even "prehistoric," for it preceded the birth of the history of these United States. Structurally, too, these walls belonged to a much earlier epoch, to the culture, the building technology that spawned Chartres and Vézelay and those medieval priories in Provence, those hermitages in Tuscany I had so often drawn, and the city walls of my home town Maastricht, completed in 1229 A.D. The partly collapsed Romanesque archway on the Wawayanda's level came as a miraculous gift: It was not a wit less Romanesque than the French ones of Tournus, Moissac and St. Savin.

As to the house across the river, we had bought it, sight unseen, a few years earlier when we spotted it, unapproachable, deep under the snow. It was the wreck of McCann's Hotel and Saloon, built around 1840. Contractors we consulted immediately diagnosed it as a terminal case, only fit to be torn down at once, and to be replaced by the "nice split-level" or the "lovely authentic Tudor" from their catalogues.

Bert Willemse at work

It must have been Providence that made us bump into Bert Willemse, a Dutch windmill builder – he had a tenfoot windmill in his front yard with a sign "Bert Willemse, Gladiolus, Carpentry" – and asked him to take a good look at our "terminal case." He climbed at once into the 1939 Buick hearse he had converted into a truck and took a good hour for a thorough diagnosis: "Structurally sound, no termites, no carpenter ants. It has to be pulled straight of course, needs new

11

roofing and some things like that, and it'll stand another hundred years."

We were ecstatic.

"How much money would be involved?"

"Can't tell," Bert said. "I charge $2.75 an hour, plus materials of course."

McCann's was irresistible. It stood there in its gaunt dignity, a bit out of kilter, on the banks of the Wawayanda, the spitting image of the dark river that careened below my great-grandfather's kitchen window on the Belgian border. The hills around, the apple orchards also, were the mirror image of those of my childhood. The house had been built into the landscape instead of sitting on top of it. It had something primeval and earthy, rooted inward about it. Our "garage" had a dirt floor inlaid with horse shoes and nails; it had once been McCann's smithy.

It all seemed to click with an aesthetic sense we shared from the very beginning: a love of gulls and clouds and meadows and simple things, preferably hand-made unpretentious things ennobled by time and love. You may still find this comfortable, warm austerity in some old Shaker house or a Quaker Meeting Room in rural Pennsylvania. Our taste seemed closely related for some reason to two basic aspects of classical Japanese esthetics: *wabi* and *sabi*. Wabi stands for an utter simplicity, a voluntary poverty of means, a chaste absence of any sign of conspicuous consumption, definitely non-Gucci, contre-Trump. Sabi refers to the charm of the agedness of things: a beloved old chair, a Victorian ceramic bowl, broken long ago, not discarded but respectfully glued together, may have gathered powerful sabi. The Harris tweed jacket I had made in Aberdeen around 1937, elbows mended, radiates sabi, and is treasured as such.

Our house and Pacem have plenty of both, wabi and

Right: The Hand of Suffering, of Agony
Above: Detail of the hand; a stigmata of blood and tears

The Unkillable Human *came about on my return from Hiroshima, where burned into a concrete wall I saw the shadow of the fellow human evaporated the moment the Bomb struck. Through the empty negative – mere flames of steel – one sees the Human rising like a Phoenix from its ashes*

REPLICAS: *Peace Park, Harrisburg, Pennsylvania; Penn State University; The Dandelion Trust, England; Nagoya, Japan; Sarajevo, Bosnia*

sabi, not as a device, not as a principle but as a given – plenty of what comes naturally must be inseparable from the inner life we share so closely. Returning from European trips, with portfolios full of drawings, we have come home again.

We were both born in Holland, Claske in The Hague, I on the southernmost tip of that small country – the thin appendix that lies squeezed between the Belgian and German borders. I have written elsewhere about this remarkable spot, where three countries, four cultures, and four languages interact – Dutch, Flemish, French, and German – where you are somewhat of a polyglot by the time you enter grade school, and where both World Wars exploded.

Still, without recapitulating some of the background, the story of our transreligious sanctuary, Pacem in Terris, would lack its very roots. I seem to be, by birth, a borderline case, a life-

14

long jumper across borders – national, cultural, religious, and linguistic frontiers that are not denied but made suggestive, inviting to be joyfully crossed. I experienced very early in life that people across the border, whatever their beliefs, whatever their ways of frying potatoes, are as human as I am, and as mortal, and that each one has an inner life of his own.

Pacem in Terris jumps across well-guarded borders, describes itself as "transreligious," which falls outside the categories of both "interfaith," and "ecumenical." It is even less a syncretistic scrambling together of symbols, concepts, and rituals of the various religious traditions. It fully respects each one of these traditions, its beliefs, its symbols, its liturgies, but is rooted in an inner experience in which these traditons converge; the word-walls that divide them become permeable on a

Lament of War, steel and glass, height 10 feet

15

level of that inner life that language lacks the tools to express. Here insights that clash in the chill of the brain seem to fuse easily in the warmth of the heart and beget a religious orientation to life as such, to Existence as the Mystery of Mysteries.

This inner life, in my case, must have been predetermined by having started on the very spot where on August 4, 1914 – I was five years old – our twentieth century started in earnest.

Left: Pope John, Deadly ill, 1963.
Above: Albert Schweitzer at 87, in Gabon Republic, Africa

The Kaiser's armies invaded Belgium, half a mile from our doorstep. The German field guns booming just across the border set our house a-tremble. From my fifth to my ninth year, I watched from our windows the endless files of fugitives

17

fleeing their burning villages, wounded and dying soldiers on pushcarts and trucks crossing the border into our neutral Holland, a wretched advance guard of those millions who would follow all through this century.

I had been born in 1909, the fateful year Louis Bleriot became the first nonbird ever to fly across the Channel, not realizing that his feat would mark the birth of a brand new era in which humans would fly across the Atlantic for a business lunch in Piccadilly, and across the Pacific for a symposium in Bangalore, to snap pictures of their loved ones against Himalayan backdrops, or to throw atom bombs on Japanese cities.

I was in second grade when I spotted a little German biplane above our schoolyard, saw the pilot look down in his open cockpit, all leather cap and goggles and, unaware of having penetrated our neutral airspace, drop the bomb. It landed close to where I was standing, but failed to explode.

Thanks to a sequence of such merciful failures, I outlived almost the full length of the twentieth century, albeit afflicted by an incurable allergy to war and physical violence. I even managed to survive that flock of howling demons, incarnations of Evil – Hitler, Stalin, Mao, and their ghoulish ilk – who massacred millions in this frightful century that was, however implausibly, also the century of Gandhi, Schweitzer, Daisetz Teitaro Suzuki, Bede Griffiths, Martin Luther King, Jr. Pope John XXIII, among so many lesser-known exemplars of being fully human. They had answered the question "What does it mean to be Human?" with their very lives – this being the central question to which all other ones, whether political, economic, religious, or artistic, are secondary.

Three of these exemplars of what, for once, is correctly called "human nature" I had the unforgettable privilege to meet, even to draw: the Protestant doctor, Albert Schweitzer; the Buddhist sage, D. T. Suzuki; and, above all, that extraordinary Catholic, Pope John XXIII.

Left: Daisetz Teitaro Suzuki, 1953

19

The fairies on duty around my cradle could not have expected this sequence, for the family in which I grew up lived on its little agnostic island in the fiercely Catholic ocean of our borderland. My father's credo was, "If you live a decent life, you don't have to fear, God or no God, the hereafter – if any."

He lived his credo with uncompromising honesty and simplicity but I failed to inherit his agnostic temperament, and I came to absorb, by sheer osmosis, the ubiquitous symbols of the Catholic culture of my childhood. They seemed to whisper answers to those early riddles: "Who am I? What am I doing here? Who is that God they constantly praise or thank or curse? Why did my pet rooster die? Where is he now? What is it 'to die'?"

Had I been born in Bombay I might have absorbed Hindu symbolism with equal eagerness. But on our Belgian border, cast-iron crucifixes and sky-blue Madonnas in their whitewashed shrines stood on every crossroad. I vaguely felt they were pointing at some mysterious Reality that transcended the humdrum preoccupations of our provincial town. These symbols, beacons in the Catholic ocean, signaled first intimations of Meaning, made me into some kind of self-styled Catholic, a totally free, unaffiliated one who, in contrast to his schoolmates, escaped all conditioning and indoctrination by the joined forces of Jesuits, Franciscans, and Dominicans in which our town abounded.

Since no one "explained" the symbols to me, they remained undistorted, free – as symbols must be – to speak directly to the heart. I now see my odd "Catholicism" as the mythical poem I wove out of candlelight, Gregorian chant, Verdi's *Requiem*, the *Agnus Dei* of Bach's B-Minor Mass as played by our local orchestra and sung by heavenly choirs of angels escaped from the altar pieces of the Flemish masters like Jan van Eyck, born five hundred years ago in our borderland.

Right: On our Belgian border cast-iron crucifixes stood on every crossroad

I must have been about twelve when I came to add a symbol all my own to the official iconography.

TWO

A few miles to the East, on the German border, nuns were constantly herding little children meekly mumbling their *Ave Marias* through a famous Calvary consisting of fourteen grottos built in the nineteenth century of fieldstone and cement. In each of these, a polychromed plaster sculpture depicted a scene of the Passion, the tormented Christ surrounded by sobbing, hand-wringing women in acid green and magenta tunics, their bulging eyes rolled heavenward. In one of the last grottos of the sequence, they sustained a swooning Virgin Mary, her sky-blue cloak undone, her heart pierced by swords. It was sentimental, melodramatic, a little sickening, and yet, through all the years of beastly massacres, gulags, and gas chambers that followed, it often came back to me, this Way of the Cross that was never further away than the next newscast. Against all esthetic odds, the symbol remained all too relevant to our human condition.

That there was no fifteenth station in the Calvary – that the Resurrection was missing puzzled me. Wasn't the Resurrection the very point of the Passion story? Had he not risen? For on Easter Sunday, with all the church bells clanging, a solemn procession wound its way through our streets celebrating his Resurrection with gold-stitched velvet banners, brass bands blowing slow, pious march tunes, a hundred angels flapping tulle wings, men in white albs swinging incense burners, devout notables in top hats holding candles,

Left: Death and Transfiguration, *also named* Resurrection, *corten steel, height 8 feet*

23

and the bishop shuffling under a golden canopy carrying the Host in its radiant monstrance.

"He is risen! He is risen!" they seemed to sing in unison with the heavenly choirs, and I saw him rising, a skylark in the luminous Easter sky...the Son of Man, the Unkillable one....

The next morning he was still hanging there on that black cross on the Cathedral wall.

What had gone wrong?

I must have been about twelve when I came to add a symbol all my own to the official iconography. In the local newspaper I saw the photograph of an almost two-thousand-year-old stone carving of a fish. It had just been unearthed in Rome's catacombs. According to the caption, the fish – *ichtos* – was the oldest symbol of Christ.

It was unavoidable in a town as Catholic as ours that I caught some talk about the Church as the "Mystical Body of Christ." I had no idea what that might mean, but it kept resonating in me as an organ chord until "Mystical Body" and the ancient Fish fused into a single image, that of a gigantic Fish. Each one of its numberless scales carried a human face. All of humanity was peering at you from the Fish's scales.

On evening walks my imagination let the Great Fish take off from a huddle of old houses around the Basilica, built a thousand years ago on the ruins of a Roman Jupiter temple. I saw the Fish rise into the night sky, saw it cross the river Meuse to sail through the interstellar spaces in the direction of the constellation Orion.

The image never faded. Many years later when I read in Kegon Buddhist writings about the "radical interdependence of all phenomena in the Universe," I met my Cosmic Fish in Chinese Buddhist garb. It had become transcultural, transreligious, embodiment and symbol of that radical interde-

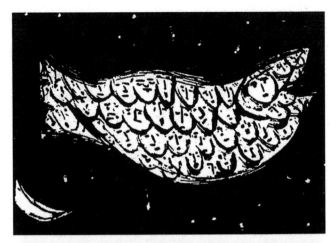

"A symbol all my own, added to the official iconography... the first icon I ever made."

pendence – to the point of mutual interpenetration – of all living things on earth and in the cosmos, a seventh-century preview of what we now give names like "deep ecology": the Oneness of the Many, the Manyness of the One.

It may well have been this Cosmic Fish that kept me from ever joining any church, sect, or Zen center, any circumscribed in-group. It made me into the loner whose single allegiance seems to be transreligious, to the All-Encompassing Fish, throughout a long life that has almost flashed by. It was the first icon I ever made. Through the years I have drawn the Cosmic Fish, painted it, engraved it, sculpted it in stone, in wood and steel, fired it on stained glass.

I never breathed a word about my Fish to anyone, but had to share its secret with my bosom pal Ernest on our day-long hikes through the almost-Tuscan hills that straddled the Belgian border. I also confided to Ernest how I could not imagine myself learning a catechism by heart, going to confession according to a laundry list of mortal and venial sins, going to Communion as a Sunday "duty."

In his innocence Ernest betrayed some of my secrets in the confessional. The priest, horrified, lost no time warning Ernest's parents against the dangers to his immortal soul by friendship with an unbeliever, or worse, a heretic.

I was more traumatized than I can tell. It was not only the end of the long hikes; it ended my unrequited love affair with the Holy Mother. I would stay on my side of the border.

Right: The True Self, *mirrored in the river, steel and glass, height 8 feet*

*Art is the tool that brings me in total
touch with the innermost workings of life,
inside and around myself.*

THREE

I was seventeen when I entered medical school without any enthusiasm whatsoever. My role models were neither the paunchy merchants of our town nor my uncles, the jovial gastro-enterologist and the stiff, formal pediatrician. The local artists were my idols – the shabby poet, the emaciated pianist who survived on Scriabin and Prokofiev, and above all, the painters. But Mother knew best. Gently but irresistibly she pushed me into Utrecht University's medical school, convinced that I was predestined to become the gastro-enterologist's successor.

As best I could, I sabotaged cutting up live frogs and dead humans soaked in formaldehyde. I skipped classes and instead gate-crashed courses in art, in Advaita, Buddhism, Taoism, and Sufism, until I could not help but feel that What Really Matters, the really Real, was equally translucent in the Upanishads, in Meister Eckhart, in Rumi, Dionysius, Ramakrishna, and Chuang Tzu. I no doubt read them superficially – I was only nineteen – yet they supplied me with the nutrients on which I could survive. They did not confuse me at all. They did not even, I felt, contradict one another, whatever their jargon. Beyond all concepts and dogmas they all seemed to point at the same Mystery of Mysteries: of being-here-at-all, of sheer Existence, and of the experiential, all-encompassing oneness of this Mystery in

Left: The Mahayana Buddhist Trinity: Trikaya, steel, 8 x 8 feet. The three elements are Dharmakaya, Sambogakaya, Nirmanakaya

29

its infinite diversification. None contradicted St. John's "Light that lightens everyone come into the world." On the contrary, they shared it, just held forth, each in its own sacrosanct cultural dialect, about this Factor X that stamps us as human. They all agreed, however, about some built-in assignment in us humans to transcend the limits of our separate little egos – each one isolated in its airtight bag of skin – if ever we are to become aware of our true place in the fabric of the Whole. No need at all to join anything whatsoever, to submit to the pretensions, the coercions of any one of these ruthlessly competing collectivized in-group egos, of churches, denominations, sects, each one loudly claiming its exclusive corner on Truth/Reality.

A professor of mathematics at our university wrote a pamphlet on Zen, which at the time, in 1926, was unheard of in the West. I still see its yellow cover in front of me, that little broadsheet that struck me as a bolt of lightning. When at last, in the forties, the Zen writings of D. T. Suzuki began to appear in English translation at Riders Ltd. and Luzac's in London, I read and reread them. They made me feel as if I had parachuted into an unknown landscape in which I recognized every hillock, every tree, as if I had known it forever.

"The spiritual life is pain raised beyond the level of mere sensation," wrote D. T. Suzuki wisely. Years later, when I asked him how he would answer the question "What is Zen?" he said, "Zen is what makes you ask the question."

Right: I made this Resurrection Cross many years ago, found it incomplete, then, suddenly, placed it in this Zen circle it demanded. The inscription on the cross reads, "Do not seek me here, for I am risen. I am the living center of the heart."

In D. T. Suzuki's *Introduction into Zen Buddhism* – I bought it exactly fifty years ago – I found as a footnote the legendary story of Zen's origin: "When the Buddha was preaching his 'Flower Sermon' to an assembly of his disciples, he did not speak a word. He just held up a

30

flower and remained silent. None of his disciples understood, but Mahakasyapa looked at the flower, at the Master and smiled. Zen had been born."

Bodhidharma, who in the sixth century brought Zen from India to China, "defined" Zen – I edit it slightly – as: *A special transmission of That Which Matters outside of all scriptures, not depending on words or letters but pointing directly at the human* hsin [Chinese "mind/heart"] *making us see into our true nature, our Buddha Nature.*

There is little to add to these descriptions, except that on that page in the old little book I had scribbled these riddlesome words: "Art is the tool that brings me in total touch with the innermost workings of life, inside and around myself."

Could this be what Hui Neng in the seventh century expressed in the words: *The meaning of life is to see?*

Could these be seeds that many years later took form as Pacem in Terris?

In midstream I escaped from medicine and landed in dentistry. It was a painful compromise, moreover barely acceptable at home, but I felt dentistry to be more neutral – that it would allow me the time I needed to think, to draw, to paint, to write, for that was what I obviously was born to do. Eventually – and I still wonder how – I got some degrees, first in Belgium, then from the Royal College of Surgeons in Edinburgh, and finally a D.M.D. in Pittsburgh, where I even taught oral surgery while painting passionately, getting a First Prize at the Carnegie Institute, followed by my first one-man show at the long-defunct Contemporary Arts Gallery in New York, on Fifty Seventh Street, in 1942. Many would follow.

Left: Ouroboros, the serpent biting its tail, oldest symbol of eternal life, of life sustaining itself, carved in white oak and black locust, 8 feet in diameter

gothic

Rain was clattering on the roof, bolts of lightning hit the surf. Time stopped, time began.

FOUR

During World War II, I served with the Dutch-East Indies government in Australia, drew Australians, kangaroos and eucalyptus trees, and painted landscapes. I returned eventually to America and set up a practice in New York, at Thirty-Three East Sixty-Fifth Street with the emphasis on oral surgery. I never worked more than two or, if unavoidable, three days a week; I called it "my economic anchor." The rest of the time I drew, painted, and wrote in my loft on the corner of Bleecker Street and Sixth Avenue. It was the top floor of the two-story ramshackle building, still surviving, where according to legend, Edgar Allen Poe once sat writing. In 1953 my son Lukas was born. He was two years old when we took a boat to Europe, where I planned to draw and paint for at least a few months. In the ten days it still took to cross the Atlantic, I revised and corrected the manuscript of my first book, *Open Wide, Please,* a self-mocking "autodental biography," written by a Dr. Frank Fredericks, illustrated by Frederick Franck. It reached three printings in England, but was never published in the States.

I was sure that I would never be able to decipher its messy, scribbled manuscript unless I could dictate it right then and there. At the Amsterdam Stedelijk Museum, while discussing my impending exhibition, I was given the phone number of a typist they often called upon when they needed

35

someone who could take English dictation straight into the typewriter. I contacted her and started to dictate. It was on September 18, 1955, a record-breaking hot Sunday, and I suggested, after a few hours of dictation in her sweltering attic, driving to a beach close by for a few hours and continuing when it had cooled off a bit.

It was just a twenty-minute drive to Bloemendaal Beach, but before we reached it the sky had turned charcoal grey. The moment I stopped on the parking lot the thunder storm exploded in full fury.

"Sorry, bad luck!"

But she sat there, eyes wide open as in a trance, staring ecstatically into the cloudburst, at the lightning flashes in the black sky.

"Ah! Look! Look! How beautiful! Mind if I go for a walk?" She had already kicked off her shoes and was out of the car, her long, thin feet trudging through the wet sand. All I could do was join her. Gulls dove into the wild surf, rose, staggered white-winged into the black sky.

"Ah! Look! See those gulls?"

She stood there, straight as a pine tree in the cloudburst, transfixed, pointing at the waves, the birds, the vertical flashes of lightning, her thin face streaming with rain.

Above and right: I found these yellowed photos we took of each other in 1955. Obstacles to our trans-Atlantic love affair seemed insurmountable. We walked down that country lane, saying goodbye forever!

36

"Such a gothic face!" flashed through my head. Van Eyck? Chartres? Reims? Anne of Aquitaine?

"Is your first name Anne?" I shouted against the thunder. She stood there in her trance, head tilted back.

"No! No! Claske!"

Friesian! Gothic! It fitted. *Coup de foudre,* or "bolt of lightning," the French call it, correctly.

"Do you know who you are?" I screamed against the thunder.

"What do you mean? Ah!" A huge gull shot by at eye level.

"Do you know who you are? You see as I see! Nobody, nobody ever sees what I see, as I see! You see! Never happened before. You are the one, we belong together, Claske!"

Soaked, we trudged back to the rented car, hand in hand. Rain was clattering on the roof, bolts of lightning hit the surf. Time stopped, time began.

> *expecting her to come*
> *how often*
> *have I wandered on the*
> *beach*

...says an ancient Japanese poem.

She had come!

The hand follows obediently what the eye percieves

FIVE

Almost half a century later, we still walk hand in hand. There are still countless moments when suddenly all is new, all is sheer miracle seen through our synchronized eyes: people, mountains, a flurry of sparrows, a tortured tree, a spastic child.

I became more and more aware of the immense difference between seeing the world around me and merely looking-at it. Every cow, every dog can look-at things and beings; only we humans can *see*. Claske had that human gift of seeing. We shared literally Hui Neng's insight: "The Meaning of Life is to see." Life disclosed its own Ultimate Meaning, not by thinking, not by debate, but by sheer seeing: it became translucent! On that September day forty-five years ago, life started. I was forty-six, she thirty-seven. All that happened before had been mere overture.

Soon – it must have been a predestined part of life's scenario – Claske joined me in the dilapidated loft across from Our Lady of Pompeii on Bleecker Street. The day she arrived, she cleaned it, put flowers everywhere, made it into a home, our home, pervaded day and night by the subtle bouquet of fragrances that rose through the old floor from street level, from Ruggiero's Fish Market, Vicente's Garden Fresh Produce, and Salvatore's Pizzeria on the corner.

I painted, drew, and wrote furiously, still had my yearly one-man show on Fifty-Seventh Street in reputable galleries like Georgette Passedoit's, who also showed Marsden Hartley, and Lilienfeld's, who featured Lionel Feininger, and later on Madison Avenue: the F.A.R. Gallery and Waddell's – by now all forgotten, as are the good reviews Howard Devree, chief critic of the *Times,* gave me, often with a reproduction on the art page. Exhibitions followed in Paris at Drouant David in the Faubourg St. Honore, at Visconti and Benezit, at Benador in Geneva, Delbanco in London, the Amsterdam Stedelijk Museum. My first book on drawing, *My Eye Is in Love,* got the *Art in America* Fiftieth Anniversary Award, and I received an honorary doctorate in Fine Arts from the University of Pittsburgh – that D.F.A. made up for the D.M.D. I was never quite comfortable with. It was followed in 1973 by *The Zen of Seeing: Seeing/Drawing as Meditation,* which is still in print and has sold – to my astonishment – far over a quarter of a million copies.

I was getting somewhere at last. I hadn't made it yet, but I was going somewhere, I told myself. Was it Claske's presence that did it? Her unerring instinct for what was a hundred percent authentic and what might be a little less? There must have been a connection between that instinct and my unease about the "somewhere" I was going.

Was I perhaps betraying something, something basic? I began to wonder about it, and about the "art world." Did it really exist, that "art world"? Was it a world? Or was it no more than a competitive subculture of our overarching Disneyland culture, a racetrack of egos on the make? Had I just lost my way into it?

That "something basic," could it be precisely the quality that in music, in painting, and in poetry had moved me to the core, from early childhood?

I knew Rainer Maria Rilke's *Stundenbuch,* his *Book of Hours,* by heart. Whole sections of it came back to me at critical moments. This was such a moment. I translate it

Right: I knew, for sure, where my drawings came from: The pen became the seismographic needle that traced down the tremors on the retina

40

from the German:

> *quench these eyes,*
> *yet they will see thee*
> *plug these ears,*
> *yet they will hear*
> *and without feet,*
> *I will go to thee*
> *and without arms,*
> *embrace thee. . .*

It pointed at this "something" in art that moved me to tears and that seems to well up irresistibly from the depth of the artist's being, light-years away from all concerns with trends, gallery circuits, marketing. It did not worry about "personal style," was not obsessed with "identity," with "being of one's time," even less with that inflated originality for originality's sake that dominated the "art scene."

I had a double exhibition on Madison Avenue, drawings at the F.A.R. gallery, paintings at Waddell's. They went very well. But at their end I stood there, looking at my canvases, semi-abstract, many of them jumbo size, sold and unsold, standing against opposite walls of the gallery.

Where did this work come from? Whose was it?

I knew for sure where my drawings come from: The hand follows obediently what the eye perceives. I let the reflex happen, let the tremors on the retina travel through every cell of my body on their way from eye – yes, via the heart – to the hand. The pen becomes the seismographic needle that traces the tremors on the retina. It traces a graph, and that graph is my drawing, as authentic as my thumb print.

Painting – however intertwined it is with drawing – is a totally different process. The moment you pick up your brush, you become the latest in a line of predecessors that started somewhere in the grey past, via the Renaissance then

Cezanne. Here the line seems to have split up, spawning one "avant garde" after the other, begetting the Fauves, Matisse, Braque, Picasso, the Surrealists, the German Expressionists, the Abstract Expressionists, until every brush-wielder of this century, obsessed by the superstitious myth of "progress," had to try to do something really "New! New!" and, dizzied by cascades of influences, produced the potpourri of stylistic debris that chokes the galleries of Fifty Seventh Street, Madison Avenue, Soho, the Rue de Seine, and the Ginza, mirroring the nihilism that pervades our society. Zenith of the myth of "progress," or nadir of what art had aspired to, ever since Lascaux?

I stood there trembling.

What only yesterday I had been so proud of suddenly filled me with despair. I could have destroyed it all, then and there! The realization destroyed, however, the gallery artist in me forever.

What on earth had been the original impulse that made me start drawing and painting so long ago? How did I get here?

I was in shock when all of a sudden I saw myself in the little tea garden called in elegant French "Les Champs Elysees," "The Elysian Fields," on the outskirts of my home town on the Belgian border.

Mother and her friend, "Aunt" Clemence, were chatting over tea; my brother was playing in the sandbox. He must have been about three or four, and I six or seven. On a ramshackle podium a trio was passionately playing waltzes and romances. I remember them as a sharp picture – the squat little lady harpist with her bottle-shaped legs, the balding violinist, Monsieur Forgeur, with his pince-nez, and the cellist, gaunt Mr. Frere. How do I, eighty-three years later, recall their names? The little elegiac melody they were playing, as if they were rehearsing it for a huge, distinguished

43

audience, I can still whistle.

I can feel again my almost religious awe for these three music makers, these extraordinary adults, in whom what I would call now the "artist-within" had survived. I managed to escape mother's supervision, crossed a little bridge over a brook, and came into a vast meadow. The vibrato of the violin, the whining of the cello, the arpeggios of the harp became softer and softer as I lay down, safely incommunicado in tall grass. It was very still. Suddenly a big bumblebee started to buzz around my head. I dared not

move, but from the corner of my eye I saw it land on the purple flower that almost touched my face. It started to suck and at that moment it happened: The flower disappeared, the bee disappeared, and so did I. All that remained was an awareness of light, as if I were staring straight into the sun. I don't know how long it lasted; it was timeless. Then, suddenly, I saw the flower again; it looked huge; it almost touched my eye. The bee was gone. All that remained was an all-encompassing bliss.

I must have touched the Untouchable, the Unsayable. I must have been as close to Reality as I would ever get, forever hungry to live that bliss again. The artist-within had been awakened.

Who is the artist-within?

The nineteenth-century French essayist Auguste Sainte Beuve wrote: "With every child a poet, an artist is born who dies young and is survived by an adult."

This short-lived artist must be the artist-within, the only authentic one who in some of us seems to survive against all odds. It is this artist-within I hold responsible for

The Eagle, the Condor and the Dove, 1998/99

turning me into the compulsive image-maker who outlived the gallery artist, and who goes off the deep end if he can not

draw, paint, or make another steel icon for Pacem in Terris. If neither Cezanne, Matisse, Mondriaan, nor Braque were my patron saints, who were? Who else but those timeless, obsessed draftsmen whose eye was desperately in love with life, with the ecstasy of seeing: Rembrandt, Breughel, Dürer, Goltzius, Guercino, Goya, Pascin, Kollwitz, Schiele, Klimt, Sengai, and Picasso at times, when he was not fooling himself and his audience. They had followed the irresistible impulse to draw what they saw, to let every line, every dot go through their every cell on the way from eye to hand. What all these compulsive draftsmen obviously had in common was to see, to see life first-hand, in constant wonder. Art had not been their compulsion to "self expression," to glorification of the inflated little ego. Art had been their zazen; drawing had been their tool, their koan to lay bare the core, to touch the Self, the Real in which we are and have our being.

I did not touch a brush for years, but drew as if my life depended on it. It did! When, years later, I started to paint again I had forgotten all about galleries, exhibitions, reviews. I drew and drew – and still draw – skies, people on New York streets, in museums, on beaches, in my native Holland, in Belgium, France, Italy, Japan, and Africa. When I draw from the car, Claske, at my side, is silent. She never disturbs me; she is all eye. She may silently point at something my eye might have missed.

The late Nanrei Kobori Roshi at Daitokuji in Kyoto, the great calligrapher and most revered friend, made me happy when he said: "Yes, drawing is your zazen, you are a twentieth-century Sengai!"

Left: Claske, 1999, a few wrinkles courteously overlooked

Lambarene 1959

I had once admitted to Clara how I often felt private practice to be "no more than a kind of shopkeeping with humanitarian pretensions."

SIX

Meanwhile I kept my precarious economic anchor in place on East Sixty Fifth.

One of my patients was a distinguished and gifted South African woman, Clara Urquhart. She had friends like Nehru, Adlai Stevenson, and Albert Schweitzer, whom she visited regularly in his legendary jungle hospital on the Equator on her trips from Johannesburg to her London flat. Clara told me that Dr. Schweitzer had complained that his hospital badly needed an oral surgeon. She literally challenged me, "Why don't you do something about it!"

I had been fascinated by Schweitzer ever since my father took me – I must have been twelve – to hear him play Bach's great Toccata and Fugue on the famous organ of the Saint Bavo in Haarlem, in the Netherlands. I read his book *On the Edge of the Virgin Forest* in 1924 when I was fifteen, and happened to be a post-graduate student at Edinburgh's Royal College of Surgeons when I attended the prestigious Gifford lectures he gave at Edinburgh University in 1937.

I had once admitted to Clara how I often felt private practice to be "no more than a kind of shopkeeping with humanitarian pretensions."

"This is your chance to stop shopkeeping for a while," she joked.

Left: Albert Schweitzer at 86 at his piano

"And my chance to draw Africa, the jungle, the people, the *Grand Docteur* himself. I'll talk to Claske about it."

49

I did, scrounged together the needed equipment, and in 1958, with Claske in the improvised role of operating-room nurse, spent most of the next three years in Lambarene, draining the abscesses and setting the broken jaws of the steady stream of patients arriving without let-up in their dug-out canoes from far up and down the Ogowe River. As the only oral surgeon in a thousand-mile radius, unpaid, as were the other doctors on Schweitzer's staff, I was anything but shopkeeping. But I found time to draw the jungle, its inhabitants, the poor mutilated humans in the leprosarium who would hide when they spotted a camera-toting visitor trying to take snapshots, but felt honored when I asked them to pose for me. I drew *le Grand Docteur*, of course, many times.

On our third trip to Africa – I tell our Lambarene adventures in detail in my books *Days with Albert Schweitzer* and *African Sketchbook* – Claske and I were at last legally married on the SS "Atlantic" of the American Export Lines by its Captain Christiansen. The formality had no nefarious effects on the love story that a few years later would give birth to Pacem in Terris, our sanctuary. It was to be our last stint in Lambarene. Claske contracted severe tropical dysentery, which made us return home for treatment.

A selection from over a hundred of my Lambarene drawings, in the collection of the Albert Schweitzer Institute for the Humanities at the Choate School in Wallingford, Connecticut, has been touring colleges and universities and is at present in Europe for similar exhibitions in Munich, Bremen, and Weimar.

Back in New York I somehow managed to continue what had survived of my all-too-part-time practice. On weekends we drove our rattling Studebaker to beaches where I drew sandpipers, gulls, and sunbathers, or to the Catskills for cows, landscapes, and trees – and fell in love with the venerable remains of McCann's Hotel.

Right: Le Grand Docteur *and his retinue*

McCANN'S HOTEL AND SALOON 1959

He loved that river. It challenged him to build a dam. He boasted that all the Willemses before him had built dams and dikes for at least a thousand years!

SEVEN

Three months after Bert Willemse went to work, McCann's had awakened from a century-long coma. There was still much to be done when we had to return to Africa for what was to be our last stint at Lambarene. I left Bert three thousand dollars, saying, "See how far you get." We shook hands on it.

McCann's meanwhile had become Bert's passion. We didn't talk much, didn't have to. We understood each other by a kind of nonverbal telepathy, and so not only did he salvage the weathered oak of the three-seat outhouse to grace the stairwell, but in our absence he improvised the monumental stone stairs to the Wawayanda. He loved that river. It challenged him to build a dam. He boasted that all the Willemses before him had built dams and dikes for at

Left: Sketch of McCann's circa 1958
Right: Photograph of side entrance of McCann's in original condition

least a thousand years! He had already constructed a wooden contraption that could serve both as a flat-bottomed boat and as a sled to carry the rocks he dug up from the riverbed. Held together by the concrete he mixed in his wheelbarrow, those rocks became the dam that created a majestic waterfall and a fine swimming hole for my son Lukas and his friends.

Someone – we suspected a grumpy neighbor – must have denounced Bert's dam. A harsh letter arrived from Albany's Conservation Department ordering us to blow up the "unlawful obstruction of a stream" at once. I wrote, pleaded by phone, sent drawings to show the spillgates Bert had constructed to allow trout and carp to pass through without the slightest impediment. Couldn't the Department send someone to inspect it? The "someone" sent from Albany, got off his Harley Davidson, all frowns and hostility. He strode to the dam, bumped into Bert, and growled:

"You built this? Wow!"

"Yup," said Bert.

"By yourself?"

"Yup."

"Gee!" said the engineer. "Some job! Would be a sin to blow that up! Great job, Mister!"

We received a retroactive permit. Prophets of doom predicted that the first winter flood of the Wawayanda would sweep Bert's dam away.

"Let it try!" he taunted. Thirty years later it is still there, as good as new, even a little better with its patina of moss.

Right: "Would be a sin to blow that up! Great job, Mister!"

.....we made the discovery that would determine the rest of our lives.....

EIGHT

That spring we started to emigrate from Bleecker Street, spending our weekends in the still unfinished house on the Wawayanda, letting down our European roots deep into our four acres of American earth. When fall came and the leaves, yellow, orange, and vermilion, were twirling down into the black Wawayanda, we made the discovery that would determine the rest of our lives: the old mill that had become a dump.

Bill Wentworth, the old man up the road, remembered that when he was a little kid his dad had worked in that mill, carrying heavy sacks of wheat from morning until night up the four stories of its wooden super-structure, which had gone up in flames one day, long ago, just before World War I. According to Bill, the mill had moonlighted at times as a cider mill. At McCann's Tavern, the cider miraculously turned into the applejack that caused a lot of fun and fights, with someone sometimes landing in the Wawayanda. Nobody seemed to know to whom it now belonged. Joe Conklin, who lived in a ramshackle house across the tracks and was rarely sober, tried his utmost to sell it to me. It just wasn't his. At long last I did find the present owner, and after much haggling became the proud owner of an early-American garbage dump for the sum of eight hundred dollars, cash.

Ever since we have wondered: Did we find that ruin, or did it sit there, waiting for us. . . ?

I decided at once to restore the Romanesque archway first, and place a replica of a Burgundian Madonna and Child in it, if I could find an affordable one.

But I had reckoned without Pope John XXIII.

Left: Cosmic Fish, *suspended, turning in the wind over dam and waterfall, wood with mirror, 5 feet*

57

On October 12, 1962 – at the height of the Cuban Missile Crisis, in the near panic of nuclear threats and counter-threats – I happened to glance at the headlines of the *New York Times* while sauntering up Fifth Avenue to an appointment with my publisher. My eye fell on a photo of rotund Pope John XXIII opening the Second Vatican Council he had convoked. I started to read the speech he had made the day before and was so astonished, so moved by this *Vox Humana* of wisdom, of humanness and compassion, coming out of the Vatican of all places, that on the corner of Twelfth Street I turned on my heels, found a phone booth, called off my appointment, ran back to our loft and read to Claske:

> As one age succeeds another, we see that opinions follow one another and exclude each other. Often errors vanish as quickly as they rise.... People ... are evermore deeply convinced of the paramount dignity of the human person. Violence inflicted, the might of arms and political domination are of no help at all in finding a solution to the grave problems that affect them. ...
>
> In the daily exercise of our Office, we sometimes have to listen, much to our regret, to voices of persons, though burning with zeal, who are not endowed with too much sense. ... In these modern times they can see nothing but prevarication and ruin ... as though at the time of former Councils everything was a full triumph for Christian ideas and love and for the proper religious liberty. ... We feel we must disagree with these prophets of doom. ...

Left: John XXIII, ill, oil on canvas, 32 x 50 inches, Collection University of Nijmegen, The Netherlands

"This is going to be a watershed! The great spiritual event of the century! I must draw that old man whatever it costs! He must be more than a Pope; he must be a prophet!

More than a prophet, he must be a Mensch! I just have to draw him and his Council! We are off to Rome, Claske, even if we go bankrupt!"

Claske understood. She knew the Ernest story and my unhappy love affair with the Church a lifetime ago, knew those moments of nostalgia when that first love suddenly flared up. A Burgundian Madonna might set it off, or a Mass by Palestrina, a poem by Rilke, by Peguy, a novel by Bernanos, a wayside cross in Brittany, the crypt of Vézelay.

Not that it lasted long, that nostalgia. There was always a news item that neutralized it, the Vatican's condemnation of a too-creative, too-liberal theologian – Teilhard, de Lubac, Congar – or the Vatican's *Concordat* with Mussolini in the making, Italian cardinals having themselves photographed blessing the Duce's bombers taking off to erase Ethiopian villages, Spanish prelates grinning at Franco, German and Polish bishops quite at peace with Hitler's mass slaughter of Jews and Gypsies. Through the years I had come to see the beloved of my childhood ever more as an obese madam in ermine, waddling sanctimoniously through this appalling century, shaking bejeweled fingers at little girls with too-deep necklines while making eyes at politicians and hucksters, waltzing with genocidal dictators.

But here was the old man's voice out of Rome that proclaimed:

...*nowadays the Spouse of Christ prefers to make use of the medicine of mercy rather than that of severity.*

Our friends were puzzled.

"You don't really think, do you, that you can just walk into that closed shop with a sketchbook under your arm? You are not even a card-carrying Catholic! *Time, Life,* and *Look* can't even get in!" One friend sent me a pair of scarlet socks, "just in case you come back a cardinal!"

I soon found confirmed that it was easier said than done. The confab of over two thousand bishops and cardinals in St. Peter's, the Council's "*aula*," seemed impenetrable – until I penetrated it.

Like everything in my life that has ever worked out, it was sheer miracle, for whatever I planned and calculated, however cleverly, usually came to naught. Was not outliving the Mussolinis, Hitlers, Stalins, and all the other demons that haunted this century sheer miracle? Was not finding the one Claske among a few billion women sheer miracle? Wasn't it a miracle, that on that October day in 1962, in the midst of the Cuban missile crisis, the world once again on the brink of terminal disaster, I heard that calm voice speaking in Rome:

> The aim of the Second Vatican Council is to consolidate the task towards the unity of humankind...the Council now beginning rises in the Church like daybreak. It is now only dawn!

This was the Spirit speaking! Could the Church be on the point of converting itself to the Gospel it claimed to be her constitution? Had a prophet arisen to make all things new? One thing I was sure of: After John XXIII things could never be quite the same again.

"One hundred percent human!" she said, "never a false note! Popes are a dime a dozen, human beings are rare. He is a human being!"

NINE

We flew to Rome, landed at Fumicino at two in the morning, and took a taxi through a freezing drizzle to Hotel Michelangelo, as faceless as any motel in New Jersey, but closer to St. Peter's.

I woke up, pulled the curtains, saw dense rain falling on red-tiled roofs in the grisaille. Church bells were ringing all over. We had made it.

The breakfast room was teeming with bishops, florid men in purple reading *Herald Tribunes,* drinking coffee, exchanging American niceties: "Wet enough for you, Monsignor? Sure coming down, isn't it!"

In that breakfast room, I suddenly realized what I was doing there, whence came that irresistible impulse. I was there to square an account, that of a passionate love affair that had started too early in childhood and had, as too-early love affairs are apt to do, turned sour. I started at once to make the contacts I hoped would enable me to draw in St. Peter's, where that extraordinary pope and his twenty-five hundred bishops were gathered every day. I did not get very far.

How I, neither bishop, nor even that "card-carrying Catholic," could gate-crash Saint Peter's during all four of the Council's autumnal sessions from 1962 to 1965, and draw the drama, its playwright, its star actors from close by, I have described elsewhere. It is too long, too complex a story to repeat here, for I wrote *Outsider in the Vatican* around these

Left: Rome, Via della Conciliazione with St. Peter's

hundreds of drawings and later *Exploding Church,* which was also published in Britain, Holland, Germany, and Mexico. One of the reviews said about the author: "He attended the Council as a contemporary Everyman."

Indeed, an Everyman, together with Claske, his Everywoman, both loved John XXIII equally. "One hundred percent human!" she said, "Never a false note! Popes are a dime a dozen, human beings are rare. He is a human being!"

Yet this is not another book about Vatican II – I remember it in the nick of time – but about the garbage dump on the Wawayanda that was to be reborn as a transreligious sanctuary. We at once called it Pacem in Terris, after the last Encyclical Pope John XXIII wrote while dying, and in which he said:

> God has imprinted on man's heart a Law his
> conscience enjoins him to obey.

"On the human heart," he stressed, not exclusively on the paper of holy books! What could that Law be but the very Law of Life, the Dharma, the Tao, the Torah, mirrored in the

Requiem Mass, St. Peter's

human heart?

I was at work in my studio on the night of April 12, 1963, when the first summary of "Pacem in Terris" came over the radio. In my mind's eye I saw Pope John proclaim it, more vigorous than ever, the Dove of the Spirit at his side. I drew what I saw in a flash with the pipette of my ink bottle.

We may hold forth on karma, coincidence, destiny, on synchronicity, all solemn words that may be no more than synonyms for what is as awesomely miraculous as life itself. Still, such a "synchronicity" – as puzzling as any – happened on June 3, 1963, when all day long we sat listening to the radio, following Pope John's long agony, until in mid-afternoon the news came that he had died. Only then I looked through that day's mail. It contained a letter from the Vicar General of New York that read: "It has pleased the Holy Father to confer on you, in appreciation of your drawings of the First Session of the Council (they had been widely reproduced) the Medal of His Pontificate. If you will call me I shall be pleased to. . . ."

It was once more an irresistible impulse. That very night, with Pope John's medal in my shirt pocket, we flew to Rome. I had to draw him once more, a last time, on his bier.

Tenente Martelli of the Gendarmeria Pontificia, the Vatican police, who had become a friend, let me draw Pope John from close by. In the half dark, hands and knees shaking, I stood there drawing the dead man who was not dead to me, never would be, who would remain a living Presence, manifestation of the Spirit in this appalling century, the Christian bodhisattva, a fully enlightened one, who vows to decline the beatitude of Nirvana until all beings are awakened, liberated from ignorance and delusion.

Of the three old men, exemplars of the fully Human, whose religion had been neither dogmatic straitjacket nor power tool, John XXIII was the greatest.

On April 12, 1963, listening to the Proclamation of Pope John's last Encyclical "Pacem in Terris" over the radio, all too aware he was dying, I saw him in my imagination more vigorous than ever, the Dove by his side! I drew him in no time with the pipette of my ink bottle

66

At the studio of Felici, the Vatican's court photographer, I celebrated my private requiem for John XXIII. I studied a few hundred photographs of Pope John meeting sick people in hospitals, others in prisons, and at his audiences: generals in gala uniform, diplomats with their ladies in gorgeous lace mantillas, a young African boy in a T-shirt. Not a single one of those photos showed a pope. Each one showed Angelo Roncalli all eyes, in total wonder and delight: "How wondrous, how wonderful you came to see me!" I had seen him look with that same delight at doves that were brought to him during a ceremony, when he was deadly ill.

We stayed in Rome until after his funeral and the Conclave, when the white smoke rose from the Sistine Chapel announcing the election of Cardinal Montini as Pope Paul VI. I drew him at his first press audience – he looked worried.

Then we flew home.

In the half dark, hands and knees shaking, I stood there drawing the dead man who was not dead to me, and never would be

Art must be something that arises from regions fathoms deeper than the empirical ego, from the deepest recesses of the human Spirit.

TEN

The moment I saw our mill ruin again I saw in a flash the roof that, seen from every angle, would seem to fly away, the stone stairs from road level to the river's edge, the terrace to be built out of the mill's debris. I scribbled down what I saw in rough sketches that were not a groping for form, just reminders of forms that had come all by themselves, from nowhere. I already spoke of the project as "Pacem in Terris" when uncoding my scribbles with the young architect who translated them into practical architectural drawings.

Bert Willemse was to be my only helper – apart from Claske, of course, who took the job that paid for Bert's wages and for the building materials needed. We would ask no one for advice, suggestions, or money. It would, for better or worse, be our work of art, our sacred space, our act of – unlabeled – faith.

The old mill had become my canvas. Freed from the rituals and delusions of Madison Avenue, life had offered me this second chance: to say in wood, stone, steel, and earth what had moved me from early childhood, deepened over the years of living through this cruel century. The gallery artist might have died a sudden death on Madison Avenue; but the imagemaker survived, was reborn.

Bert and I started at once to dig out the rubble

Left: Matrix, steel and ceramics, 8 feet
Above: Detail

69

A sacred space, a space "outside of the rat race," an oasis of silence, of inwardness, of sanity, of sanctity

and debris, twelve hundred wheelbarrows of it. We dug by hand, as machinery might have destroyed the old walls. Meanwhile, Bert had reinforced the jagged top of the ruin's walls with a beam of concrete and steel that tied the entire structure together. We continued digging until we reached the muddy pit where the mill wheels once turned. A millstone and a scoopwheel were rescued, as was the mill's axle – which was to become the trunk of the Tree of Life mosaic in Pacem's floor – a medallion of spikes, cogwheels, and horse shoes found in the rubble and set in concrete. We noticed how the pit kept filling itself with water although there was no connection with the river. It trickled down from springs in the rocks. "An omen!" Had

Petrified Man, *scanning the skies, granite, 6 feet, (detail)*

not sanctuaries been built on sacred springs from time immemorial?

We swapped rocks from a wall between a neighbor's meadows for rolls of barbed wire. These rocks became the stairway from road level to the precious Romanesque archway and the paving of Pacem's floor. Bert started to assemble the gigantic fifty-one-foot-long diagonal wooden truss on road level. It would support the flying roof. One day, returning from New York, we were astounded. The truss was in place on its abutments.

"Rented a crane?" we asked.

"No," said Bert.

"Then how on earth did you do it?"

in meditation...

He shrugged.

"With the jacks of my truck."

We were never able to get more information out of him. It remained the secret he took with him to the grave a few years later.

When I was not building, I kept working on the sculptures, the stained glass windows, the mosaics for Pacem, and I began to feel more and more closely

related to the craftsmen of ages past: the masons, the wood- and stone-carvers, the icon-makers of centuries ago, the cathedral builders of the Middle Ages – even, all the way back, to those Cro-Magnons of Altamira and Lascaux who, thirty thousand years ago, painted murals on the rock walls of their caves.

It was as if I were taking a crash course on what the art impulse is really about: an art that is neither luxury, nor show-off, nor merchandise to be sold in shops called galleries, and even less a hobby. Art must be something that arises from regions fathoms deeper than the empirical ego, from the deepest recesses of the human Spirit. It must spring from its maker's truth, his

Right: Transcending Eagle, granite, assemblage

74

core, if it is to touch the core, the truth of the one who confronts it. Art does not seek to preach, to shock or to charm. It is not even too concerned about being liked. It can't help being what it is.

Kafka tells about a craftsman who is building a table and reflects on his making of that table as being a nothing, a nothing that is everything. This is what the cave painters may have felt when they painted those majestic animals on their rock walls, and the carvers of the lintels and capitals of Chartres and Vézelay, the Crucifix of Perpignan, the reclining Buddha of Anaradhapura. What these artists were carving was that "No-Thing" that is all that matters.

"Art is not to express personality, but to overcome it," wrote T. S. Eliott. Any Bach fugue confirms it. It is not a Mr. Bach expressing himself; it is the Unnamable expressing Itself through Johann Sebastian.

To proclaim oneself "an artist" is preposterous. To be an "artist" is not an occupation, as being a plumber, a baker, or a doctor is an occupation. It is even less a hobby.

"Artist" is an honorific. It fits Rembrandt, Rafael, Rodin, Manzu – they fully merit the honorific, as do innumerable unknowns who through the ages were authentic artists. Others who neither draw, paint, nor play an instrument can let the artist-within shine through unmistakably. The true artist is the artist-within, the Mensch within, expressing him/herself, despite all fashions, as authentically as one's DNA, EKG, or thumbprint. Looking at a Paul Klee – with whom I feel no real contact – I recognize at once his expression of the true artist-within.

Right: Exiting from Pacem

My St. Francis icon was to be that of a saint for all seasons, a trans-historical, trans-religious messenger of love of life, of nature, of the earth as sacred.

ELEVEN

As Pacem was taking shape, the ruin seemed to transform itself into a huge sculpture, a massive icon of earth, stone, and wood, partly subterranean. One could descend into it, sit down in its silence, then climb out of it, refreshed, one's trust in life, one's *joie de vivre* rekindled.

The mill's interior, too, was coming alive as a sacred space – a space "out of the rat race" that might resonate with the sacred space at the core of the human heart, a tiny oasis of sanity, or call it sanctity, in the violently churning madhouse of our world.

"Art is that which, despite all, gives hope," I carved in one of its walls.

I call my three-dimensional images in wood, stone, and steel, "icons" rather than "sculptures." The word "icon" denotes "a window on to the Sacred," the "really Real." They are symbolic forms that in their simplicity, their directness, invite to reflection, free association, and self-confrontation.

When I am asked "What does this one mean?" I answer, "If I could put it in words, I wouldn't have to make it in steel."

Symbols have something in common with jokes: You catch them or you don't.

Nothing at Pacem is "designed," nothing is "figured out." "Petrified Man Scanning Sky" was a formless pile of rocks that spontaneously took on this human form. In

Left: Seven Generations, *seven-element steel icon, 32 feet perspective*
From the Great Law of the Six Nation Iroquois Confederacy "In all our deliberations we must be mindful of the impact of our decisions on the seven generations to follow ours."

REPLICAS: *Cathedral of St. John the Divine, New York; Penn State University; Omega Institute, Rhinebeck, New York; Wainwright House, Rye, New York; Bucknell University, Pennsylvania; Peace Garden, Harrisburg, Pennsylvania; Choate, Wallingford, Connecticut; Santa Cruz, California; Bad Herrenalb, Germany; Hengelo, The Netherlands; Fundacion Elpis, Argentina; Hasselt Cultural Center, Belgium*

79

"Phoenix Rising" and in "Hiroshima, the Unkillable Human," negative and positive space played their game of counterpoint. Hui Neng's "Original Face," Cusa's "Face of Faces" took shape again and again: the human face as epiphany. The "Seven Generations" came to me as I sat doodling, mind blank, waiting for a delayed phone connection. I at once translated it into steel. There are four or five variations on the theme of the Cosmic Fish, in steel, in stone, in stained glass. One of these, in wood, floats in the sky high above Bert's dam. The "Resurrection" or "Death and Transfiguration" icon all of a sudden loomed up while I was leafing through a magazine in a doctor's waiting room, Muzak blaring. The "Black Madonna"of Newark was drawn spontaneously on the steel plate without any preliminary sketch.

The St. Francis icon that I made in 1998, about thirty-five years after Pacem was opened, came suddenly, absolutely unannounced, as I read something about the earthquake in Assisi that destroyed the Cimabue, which had moved me even more than the Giottos. It was cut directly from the rolled, ten-foot-high steel plate. Front and back fitted together by sheer grace, and the fifty bird forms followed at once as in a fever, their wing tips welded together without a moment's doubt: a typhoon of birds.

My St. Francis icon was to be that of a saint for all seasons, a transhistorical, transreligious messenger of love of life, of nature, of the earth as sacred. His hymn to his Brother Sun, his Sister Moon, his Brother Wind, his Mother Earth was the hymn of an ecological hero *avant la lettre*, singer of the Hymn for our time.

I made the icon for Pacem in Terris, but some friends decided it belonged in Assisi, resurrected after the earthquake of 1997, and so I made a precise replica. It was flown to Rome, trucked to Assisi, and donated to the Sisters of the Atonement to be part of their restored convent, and

Top left: Earth Song, *rusted steel, 4 x 10 feet*
Bottom left: Phoenix, *rising from its ashes, steel, 6 feet*

was dedicated there in October 1999.

Pacem was still unfinished when we opened it in 1966 to whomsoever wanted to climb down the stone stairs into its silence. Ever since it has been open to all – no tickets, no charge – on weekends from May to October, whenever the eight-foot Banner of Humanity is blowing in the breeze. The Banner consists of five stripes. They symbolize the five subdivisions of the one human race: brown, black, red, white, and yellow. United at the top, each one of these stripes is free to blow in the wind according to its nature. It is tubular; none of these stripes is first, none last, none on top, none at the bottom. Each stripe is double: male and female. Claske added a bright green streamer that signifies the Earth. The Banner of Humanity was not "designed" either; it just blew in from nowhere.

In Pacem's facade, I carved: "I built Pacem in Terris, an oasis of sanity, reconnecting Self and Nature. It is dedicated to Angelo Roncalli, John XXIII, Albert Schweitzer, and Daisetz T. Suzuki, prophets of human solidarity, exemplars of what is Human in everyone born human. May the Spirit soar and make us humans see our unity."

It came as a wondrous surprise that Pacem's acoustics were as outstanding as they were unplanned. Musician friends brought their violins, their oboes, experimented, speculated on the acoustic phenomenon. Might it be due to these stone walls crowned by the huge wooden soundbox of the roof?

They played and loved what they heard themselves play. It was the beginning of the annual series of chamber music concerts that in the past twenty years have regularly drawn full houses.

No one ever preaches in Pacem except Bach, Vivaldi, Mozart, Schubert, and their next of kin. They do not infringe on its silence. They make that silence audible, amplify it.

Right: St. Francis and his Birds, *steel, 10 feet high*

REPLICA: *dedicated in Assisi, October 1999*

82

Occasionally there are poetry readings and stagings of *The Death and Life of Everyone,* my contemporary variation on the medieval theme of Everyman, or *Inquest of a Crucifixion,* a contemporary Passion play. Both are timeless themes, as relevant as ever. *The Death and Life of Everyone* was premiered in Melbourne in 1972. It returned to Pacem, was performed in St. John the Divine, Trinity Church, and St. Luke's in New York, and by drama departments in the United States and Canada. In it the "Voice of God from the heavens" has been a woman's voice – often Claske's – in 1972, still a risky innovation.

Pacem has made itself available for intimate services, Protestant, Unitarian, Catholic, and Buddhist. It has been the scene of weddings for couples with a special love for Pacem, some christenings, and memorial services. Although it is only open from May to October, there is an exception on New Year's Eve, when an adaptation of a Tibetan-inspired New Year's celebration takes place, its only ritual.

A long time ago, we happened to be in Dharamsala on the eve of the Tibetan New Year. At the edge of the village a teepee-like hut of branches and leaves had been built. A solemn procession of lamas, accompanied by six-foot-long trumpets and shawms, proceeded from the main temple to the hut. An offering was placed in it and the hut was ignited.

The huge flame, burning all the sins committed in the dying year against the backdrop of the snow-clad Himalayas, was unforgettable. Could we adopt the ritual, we wondered. Warwick lacking Himalayas, we built our hut on a float moored at Pacem. The ceremony starts at The Dove, from where a candle-lit procession proceeds to the old mill. A brief reading of Eastern and Western scripture is followed by the distribution of the day's *Times,* bringer of ill tidings, torn into pieces. Each one present is asked to wrap the frustrations and sins of the past year in one of the

Left: Black Madonna and Child, *steel, 8 feet*

REPLICA: *in Day Care Center, New Community Corp., Newark, New Jersey*

scraps of newspaper and throw it into the basket passed around. The basket is placed in the hut. All bells ringing, the hut is ignited, the moorings are cut, and a forty-foot-high flame of purification careens down the Wawayanda over the dam, where it explodes into a fountain of sparks. Originally we started it for a few friends, but nowadays we receive a few hundred requests of which only a limited number, for safety's sake, can be accepted.

One night in 1982, we were awakened by sirens. Joe Conklin's dilapidated house, across the railroad tracks, an early nineteenth-century contemporary of McCann's Hotel – as old as ours – stood burning like a torch. Only the stone foundation remained. The ground around it was piled high with car and motorcycle wrecks, bedsprings in all phases of decomposition, old bathtubs on their backs, lion claws in the air. The lot was too small for a house according to the zoning law. We could buy it for a song, as number three in our collection of ruins. Volunteers carried the debris away, then built a simple cottage on the stone foundation.

We called it a "caretaker's cottage," for that category had been skipped in the zoning law. The ground around it became a "sculpture garden": "The Meadow of Signs."

The cottage, named "The Dove," was to become home to Arthur Meyer, the man sent by Providence at the right moment. Art, a Vietnam veteran, is endowed with uncommon technical versatility and creativity as carpenter, electrician, and welder. Without him, we might not have been able to keep Pacem as active – more active than ever – as we are getting older and older, and my production of new steel icons might have faltered.

Right: Poster for premiere in Melbourne, Australia 1972 of what was later re-named: "The Death and Life of Everyone."

86

THE PLAY OF EVERYMAN
FREDERICK FRANK'S RADICAL RE-CREATION OF THE 15 TH CENTVRY
DRAMA, IN THE "PACEM IN TERRIS" NEW YORK PRODVCTION
DIRECTED BY RICHARD MANN
a shout of affirmation of the human for now and the year 2000
ONE WEEK ONLY: SATVRDAY 19-26 FEBRVARY 1972   8-30 P.M.
AVGVSTINE THEATRE-CHVRCH 500 BVRWOOD RD. HAWTHORN VICT.
LIMITED SEATING . TICKETS $1⁵⁰ CAIRNMILLAR INSTITVTE.

*I see us as self-identical, while remaining
who we are, far from equal but totally
equivalent, utterly precious.*

TWELVE

There came a moment, about ten years ago, when we
began to feel that the beloved backyard wilderness be-
hind our house actually belonged to Pacem in Terris.
Slowly but surely it had grown into a second "icon gar-
den," along the unpaved, grassy footpaths that follow
the river, past the often wildly roaring waterfall over
Bert's dam, and all the way around the circular Resur-
gence Garden to the "Sacred Tree," the gigantic, three-
hundred-year-old wild cherry that holds a diminutive
white ceramic angel between its gnarled roots. We found
it there one day in memory of a young girl whose ashes
had been buried on that spot.

We landscaped our backyard very inexpensively –
by not landscaping it at all. Who were we to improve on
what nature had done so admirably! Only here and
there we mowed an island in the grass around an icon –
the "Seven Generations," for instance, with its seven ele-
ments, the "Heart of Stone," the "Resurrection Cross"
in its Zen circle of No-Thingness, *Sunyata.*

Friends cautioned us against opening up our
backyard to strangers. "Don't be foolish! They'll swarm
all over the place! They'll put graffiti on your sculptures!
Your privacy will be gone! Be reasonable!"

These warnings, well-meant, were obviously
based on the misconception that there is something

*Left: The "social mask"
opened to lay bare the True
Self, main theme of Pacem in
Terris, stone, 23 inches height*

"reasonable" about Pacem. We may not be quite sure what exactly it is, but reasonableness is not what it is based on.

Pacem seems to have created itself as a chain reaction of inspirations, an obstinate trust in what is still human in us humans despite all that assaults the Spirit. The anti-music, the inescapable din of radio and television, the oversaturation with electronic images, the uninterrupted lies of advertising tempting us to buy things we don't need are continuous assaults on the inner life, that one priceless human treasure that can not be bought and sold, but can be killed, perverted.

We defied the prophets of doom and opened the backyard to "them." And lo and behold, "they" didn't put any graffiti on anything; "they" didn't tear out a single flower or cabbage, did not encroach on our privacy, didn't even drop a cigarette butt.

From my writing table, I see "them" sauntering quietly down the paths through the high grass, pointing at an icon, puzzling maybe. A little group of boys and girls, then a teenage couple holding hands, another couple with two little girls cavorting, a trio of oldsters limping on canes. The backyard had become the meditative walk we hoped it might be.

"It is so beautiful!" they say. "Thank you for sharing this with us!" they write on the pad in Pacem and in letters that come day after day. "Unbelievable! Wow! At last an art after my heart," were the latest notes on the pad, and "This piece of earth is now a piece of art, my only church."

I stop writing, see in the distance Claske cutting off a large broccoli, picking a cucumber, a few zinnias for an old couple she may have met in the circular garden. On the bench at the Sacred Tree, people must be sitting, looking up to where its branches dissolve in the sky.

This morning a woman rang the bell, handed Claske a book of mine, asked if she could talk to me about

it, and have it autographed.

"Sorry, he is at work, I can't interrupt him now."

"I understand," the woman said, "so why don't you sign it for me; your essence must be in it as it is in everything he does."

True! The name Frederick Franck on a book cover

is the name of the company, mere trademark.

In 1965 I dedicated *My Eye Is in Love,* to "Claske, who is happy when I draw." She is still happy when I draw, still the one critic I trust unconditionally, the one in whose face I read instantly what she feels about the drawing, the painting, the piece of writing I just finished.

Claske, when I shouted on that beach: "You are the one!" it was obviously in a flash of clairvoyance. Forty-five years of tasting the fullness of life in unison, of still seeing through these synchronized eyes proves it. Moments of quarrel, at times almost violent, were always brief, for we both realized at once that the outburst was nothing but an implosion of the overloaded switchboards of two nervous systems. No sentimental rituals of reconciliation were need-

Incarnations of the Humanum, *ceramics*

92

ed, even less psychological theorizing. Just an embrace. After one of our implosions, slamming the door of Edgar Allen Poe's loft, you came up the stairs twenty minutes later, radiant, carrying the terrapin turtle you had rescued from Ruggiero's Seafood Emporium. You had already christened it "Poor No-One" and cared for it as if it were your child

until the day "Poor No-One" died.

After another switchboard malfunction, you might put a flowering branch in a bottle on my table, or a wondrous branch of a sycamore with huge leaves, knowing that I would draw it.

We were once mugged on Upper Broadway. Two men gripped me from the back, I saw a rusty knife at eye level. The third one, the "blind" one with the white cane – it was a piece of pipe – hit you on your head. You didn't faint. You let go with that bloodcurdling, piercing yell, "Paaaaauww!" you had learned as a Girl Scout and sometimes rehearsed in the country.

Working on a steel icon with Arthur Meyer

"Pppaaaaauww!" I felt the grip loosen, saw them run across Broadway. Had they taken it for a death yell?

93

Perhaps. But run they did. You had a tangerine-sized swelling on top of your head. You are not scared of bullies, of muggers...you scare them to death.

Still, you are the same woman who comes into my studio with HeShe, one of your twelve ring-doves, on your index finger. HeShe – gender in doubt – was born weak, a

bit sickly, parental care withdrawn. You raised the little white dove, tamed it by sheer tenderness. You treat your chickens, your two rabbits as the wondrous beings they are to you. You'll catch the yellowjacket on the windowsill in a towel to release it outside. You never lost the gifts of wonder and of tenderness. The woman met on that stormy beach is simply a genius at being woman, at being human.

Above: Social Mask – *the human face, closed off, steel, 5 feet*
Right: Human face, opened, revealing the self

Here then, at last, is the reply of why we transmuted a garbage dump into a sanctuary – overflow of the fullness of a life shared, of a love affair that was more than a *folie a deux.*

94

Working on my icons, I sometimes wonder if they are perhaps "conclusions" – in another medium – of drawing, as being in total touch with those thousands of human faces, trees, clouds, and animals, which distill themselves into icons.

Sometimes, drawing people in Canal Street and Chinatown, I suddenly do not see them sharply as bodies and faces but as life cycles, or call it karmas: each one once-occurring, unrepeatable, each one that particular condensation, however temporal, of the Mystery of Being. My eye, just as temporal, sees. My pen touches that life-cycle for a few seconds. I don't see "brothers and sisters!" I see us as self-identical, while remaining who we are, far from equal but totally equivalent, utterly precious. The young ones I see as oldsters, the oldsters sometimes reveal themselves for an instant as youngstrers, but all of us one-day flies, pathetically naked, both funny and pitiful.

> *The morning dew flees away*
> *is no more*
> *what remains*
> *in this world of ours?*
> —Ikkyu

If this should sound too much in B Minor, it also happens while drawing the whores and peddlers on Fulton, the cops on Maiden Lane. I feel all at once that I am drawing an Ode to Joy, to the Unkillable Human.

"The world comes to an end with the last thought; it is resurrected with the next one." It may even be true! For I spotted Chuang Tzu, resurrected, shuffling down Mott Street, looking as young after twenty-five-hundred years as I do after ninety. Of course I drew him, and I wondered: Could what appeared on my paper be the print-out, in forms, of some formless pattern of the

Meeting Chuang Tzu on Mott Street

Universe, including the tiniest of these forms, that of the one who is drawn and the one who draws?

Back to Pacem, the sanctuary of silence that does not aspire to convert anyone to anything, that neither propagates nor promotes whatsoever. On the contrary, it is a tiny safe haven from all that propagates and promotes. If it has any ambition at all, it is to be that safe-haven, a miniature sign of hope, a tiny oasis of sanity in the vortex of madness that conditions every child born human, programs it, estranges it from its potential, its vocation, to become fully human.

For a moment I was stunned. I had brushed the Way of the Cross in a frenzy, almost in shock at one of those outbursts of barbarism that is part of our daily media-diet.

THIRTEEN

A few years ago, at one of those trigger points of horror – it may have been Mogadishu that time – the images of the "Way of the Cross," indelibly etched on the inner eye in childhood, sprang to life with such urgency that I grabbed a brush. I had to give it form – black ink on large sheets of paper. Stripped to its bare essentials, it became a sequence of close-ups of the Human Face, the "Face of faces," which the fifteenth-century Christian mystic Nicholas of Cusa detected it in every human face, "veiled as in a riddle." It is also Hui Neng's Original Face, Unveiled.

My fifteen panels, ink on paper, of "Way of the Cross" became part of the collection of the Cathedral of St. John the Divine and led to this story within a story.

It started with a phone call from Des Moines, Iowa, early in 1996.

"Mr. Nims would like to speak to you. Hold on, please."

I never met Dean Nims in the flesh but for years he has been a faithful supporter of Pacem in Terris.

"Frederick, I have been thinking about your 'Way of the Cross' and your Oxherding Pictures in

Left: Frederick Franck , self-portrait ca. 1998, ink sketch on canvas

99

St. John the Divine. They touched me and I just wonder, have you ever considered translating these into stained glass? Could be wonderful, couldn't it?"

For a moment I was stunned. I had brushed the "Way of the Cross" in a frenzy, almost in shock at one of those outbursts of barbarism that is part of our daily media-diet. Years ago I had studied stained glass with Albin Elskus, renowned master in the craft, including the classical techniques of painting plain glass and firing it. I loved the medium but somehow had not worked in it for ages. This would be my chance! Was there any subject more timely than this at the end of this cruel century?

"Inspiring idea!" I said, "I know of nothing more timely to try my hand on! Let me think about it, and find out how I could do it, for I have no kilns and all that around. I'll call you back."

As I was painting those Stations of the Cross in ink, I had come to see the ancient story of Christ's Passion ever more as transcending the traditional form of the fourteen grottos on the German border. I saw it as an ongoing, transhistorical drama, still taking place every day all over the globe – as "Catholic" indeed, but in the sense of being universal, timeless in time, transreligiously valid. The *Condition Humaine,* the Way, the Truth, the Life. It addressed itself to Everyman. It transcended gender and creed. It bridged East and West. I called it the "Tao of the Cross" when I started working on its stained glass version.

Dean James Parks Morton of the Cathedral of St. John the Divine wrote about the black and white "Tao of the Cross":

> A precious moment in history that can present together the sacred images at the center of two distinct religious traditions. In this work we find the open heart of the Stations of the Cross and

Left: "The Other Shore" at night.

Left: Stained glass window, from The Tao of the Cross, Station One, Condemned to Death

Right: Stained glass window, from The Tao of the Cross, Stations Six *and* Twelve

1.

1.
The Oxherd Has Lost His Ox... (The True Self)
2.
He Espies the Ox Hoofprints
3.
He Sees the Ox, Far Away...
4.
He Catches the Ox
5.
He Has Caught the Ox... Now to Tame It...

2.

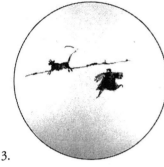

3.

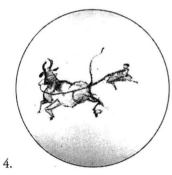

4.

5.

the quiet mind of the Oxherding series represented as accessible to all men and women...a progress of the deepest kind.

I remembered seeing a sign, "Sundog Glass Studio," just a few miles from Warwick, in Sugar Loaf, New York. I drove to Sugar Loaf and found two young women at work restoring a stained glass church window. They were clearly professionals. When I showed them reproductions of the black and white sequence I hoped to "translate" into stained glass, they were at once enthusiastic, called it a "creative adventure." Then and there we figured out the cost.

I called Des Moines and told Mr. Nims that I had found the place and the help I needed to work on the "Tao of the Cross" in stained glass.

"For me it is a labor of love," I said, "but there are considerable expenses: the materials, the firing, the leading, and finally the fabrication of the windows. I have an estimate and it is not cheap."

"About how much?"

I told him. There followed a second of silence and then, "I'll send you a check."

I couldn't believe my ears. It could only happen in America.

"Where do you plan to place these windows?" I still asked.

"We can talk about that later. Just go ahead... by the way, would you have space for them at Pacem in Terris?"

The work took a full three months. Apart from using electric kilns, I worked in the techniques Albin Elskus had taught me, techniques that have hardly changed since the Middle Ages. I would avoid the use of any

6.

7.

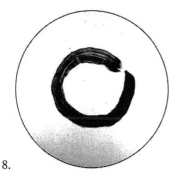

8.

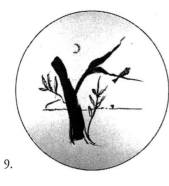

9.

industrial colored glass, would start with good quality clear window glass of various textures.

I drew the Stations on large sheets of paper. On these I outlined the pattern of segments to be painted, fired, and leaded. I transferred these patterns to the glass and cut it accordingly. There were some four hundred of these segments, each one to be painted with vitreous "enamels" and silver stain, then fired in a kiln at 1,000 to 1,250 degrees to bond the color to the glass. The color range I aimed at was subdued: grisailles and earth colors. I would avoid the standard "stained glass" gaudiness of blood-reds, sky-blues, bright yellows. Some fragments were fired again and again until the desired intensity of ochre or sienna was reached.

These three months became a retreat, a continuous meditation, a self-confrontation. Painting those fourteen close-ups of the Face of faces – Hui Neng's Original Face – I was not after elegant, decorative effects. It was a getting in touch with the quintessence of the human condition. There was in this stark sequence of fourteen scenes only one humane act, Veronica's wiping of his brow. . . perhaps there were two, if Simon of Cyrene's help in carrying the cross was an act of mercy. The rest was indignity inflicted, torture, pain, and death, until all at once – in the fifteenth station I added to the conventional fourteen – the stony heart of darkness was shattered by the blinding light of triumph over death, by the Unkillable Human. In my "Tao of the Cross," the Resurrection would not be missing.

With the Resurrection, Rebirth as its apotheosis, I felt the "Tao of the Cross" ever more as mirroring the human inner process – its dolorous maturation, its resolution as endpoint of the human pilgrimage.

While at work on it, I looked at the stained

106

6.
He Has Tamed the Ox, Rides Home on It, Playing His Flute...
7.
The Ox Has Disappeared...
8.
Both Ox and Oxherd Have Disappeared...
9.
All Things Have Become New...
10.
He Descends Into the Market Place Bestowing Blessings

glass "Cosmic Fish" I did years ago in Albin Elskus's studio and wondered how as a twelve-year-old I dreamt up this symbol of Absolute Oneness in limitless differentiation, the absolute interdependence of all Being in the cosmos.

In this three months-long meditation-in-action, this being "face to face" with the "Face of faces" I was painting, I mused on this Face of the one who "was before Abraham was."

I felt the Face must have appeared at that crucial point of our evolution when, long before Abraham was, the primitive, the anthropoid, the Naked Ape, mutated into Anthropos, the Adam of the Genesis myth. "Adam" means "human being." Still, this Adam soon proved to be all too tainted by surviving automatisms of the anthropoid, the Naked Ape. I came to see this old Adam as the predecessor of the New Adam, the Absolute Human, the one from whom the last of prehuman atavisms had dropped off, who manifested the "Human beyond description and understanding," the Human Absolute, the Absolute Human.

The epiphany of the Face as it appeared in my fifteen windows, almost primeval in their simplicity, came to me in a sudden vision, years ago in Melbourne, when I spontaneously jotted it down with my writing brush while working on a poster for *The Death and Life of Everyone*, which we were staging in St. Augustine, an abandoned church in Melbourne's outskirts. Later it was to become the logo of Pacem in Terris. To me it epitomizes the specifically unkillable Human core, the Sleeping Christ within, the Buddha Nature, the Jivanmukti of Hinduism, the Sacred Man of the Taoist sages, the Perfect Man of the Sufis, the Divine Spark.

It takes time for glass to cool down from 1,200 degrees after a kiln full of fragments is switched off. I used these

Face of faces, (Nicolas Cusa); The Original Face, (Hui Neng) *candle lit, synthetic stone, 6 feet*

intervals to work on a stained glass rendering of the Ten Oxherding Pictures, of which I had drawn an ink-on-paper version some time ago. I do not see this Parable of the Oxherd as "equal" or "equivalent," or even "analogous" to the Tao of the Cross. I see it in its profundity as a sequence of images that has proven to be a powerful catalyst and guide in meditation on the human condition ever since it originated in medieval China. The version I followed is that of the fifteenth-century Zen master Kaku-an. It had been preceded by much earlier versions, some still surviving, of five, six, and eight images. In its Far-Eastern idiom, the Ten Oxherding Pictures evoke the human journey from its still prehuman confusions and delusions to full maturation of human consciousness: Enlightenment, Awakening, Liberation.

The parable starts with the oxherd wandering in despair on a barren field. He has lost his ox, symbol of the True Self; has violated his innermost nature. The parable then traces the steps of its recovery, which culminates in the oxherd's full Enlightenment in picture number eight. Kaku-an added the two final images. In number nine the oxherd's awakened eye sees "all things having become new," and in the final picture he has become the bodhisattva, the fully enlightened one who, foregoing the beatitude of Nirvana, descends into the town square to bestow blessings and to lead those still lost in darkness and delusion to their awakening from relative "reality" to Reality.

My Parable of the Oxherd, a free rendering of Kaku-an's version, consists of ten small windows of ten by ten inches. Each window consists of three layers of glass. The outer one carries the image and the title in black and greys, fired to bond them to the glass. The second layer, the circle, is not painted, but etched; the third layer is

Left: Hand with Flower, *rising out of flood, steel, 6 feet*

slightly sandblasted, so that, when they are sandwiched together, a translucent, subtle silk-like texture is obtained, which is lost in opaque color reproductions.

Around the time I was working on these twenty-five stained glass windows, I happened to read some articles about contemporary research in neuroscience, which I mention here as they confirm, in purely scientific terms – one might say reductionist terms – the most profound intuitions of the prescientific mind. I read about the research by Paul D. MacLean, M.D., Chief of the Laboratories of Brain Evolution at the National Institutes of Health, which resulted in his description of the human brain as a triune brain, a trinity of brains, of which the most ancient and central component is the reptilian brain, surviving in us with all its 280,000,000-year-old automatisms intact and as active as ever. In the course of evolution, this reptilian brain was enveloped by, respectively, the old and the new mammalian brain. The most recent outcropping of our human brain is known as the prefrontal cortex. It proved to be the humanizing component, for it enables us – as no animal before – to be aware of our own life process from birth to death. This awareness makes it possible for us to become aware of the life process of other beings, to identify with their mortality, their joys and sorrows – the first inklings of empathy can arise; from empathy to compassion is but a step.

Could it be this capacity for compassion that is the crucial criterion of being human? Are we not born genetically encoded as humans with the potentiality to become Human against all odds? Don't we all know instinctively what it means if someone is described as being "so human," or is called "a real human being?" Is there a greater compliment than being called a real human being?

The Buddha's "Great Wisdom that is the Great

Top: Interior of Pacem in 1963, when it all began Bottom: The Birds of St. Francis in Winter

Compassion," the Christ's Impartial Love, the Agape that is Sophia are the paradigms of the fulfillment, the completion, the final maturation of the human inner process, Lodestars on our Way.

Once the twenty-five stained glass windows, large and small, were finished, they were exhibited in the St. Boniface Chapel of St. John the Divine, then in the New Community headquarters of Newark, the Paul Mellon Gallery on the campus of the Choate School in Wallingford, Connecticut, before they found their permanent home – once again with Dean Nims's support – at Pacem in Terris, in the austere, contemplative space Art Meyer built for them on the opposite shore, across the Wawayanda from the early-American dump that became a sanctuary. "The Other Shore" not only refers to its location across the river. It also intends to evoke that "other shore" across the ocean of delusion, suffering, and ego inflation of which the Buddha speaks as "Awakening," the awakening from the anger, greed, and folly of the unexamined life, the Mystery of life taken for granted.

All the icons of Pacem in Terris – I realize it at this moment – seem to evoke Awakening, Rebirth, the Resurrection of the inner life, of the Unkillable Human, of the Fullness of Life.

May all beings be fulfilled!

Coda

Having written this late at night, I had a dream of our having wandered into a party. It was a garden party.

The guests were all young. Long-legged girls and boys in black tie were dancing on a red-tiled floor. I couldn't see it all very sharply; perhaps my eyes were out of focus. I couldn't stand the music, switched off my hearing aid.

We were sitting on the edge of the lawn in two white chairs. The armrests touched. We sat hand in hand and watched.

"What are you thinking?" I asked.

"Same as you. What do you see?"

"I see us on that beach. I see you in Lambarene, sterilizing my instrumentarium. I see you in that black mantilla on the Piazza San Pietro on our way to Pope John's audience. And now I see you, your face brick red, when you had that heat stroke as we drove with little Lukas through the Mojave desert all the way to San Francisco. I see you again on Bloemendaal beach, your face streaming with rain.

"How long ago it is.... But I see it all now as if it all happened in one afternoon, one very long, glorious afternoon, and now dusk is falling.... Oh, how terribly short it was, Claske...how frightfully short....

"You remember that Indian saying, that lovers may reincarnate together?

"We are not so sure of reincarnation, are we?

"Hold my hand tighter, Claske, beloved...."

Left: Frederick and Claske in Pacem, October 17, 1999

117

Appendix

SOME RAW FACTS ABOUT PACEM IN TERRIS

Pacem in Terris – Peace on Earth – is a not-for-profit corporation under the Education Laws of the State of New York. It received its charter on July 31, 1970, and is governed by a Board of Directors as required by the Charter, assisted by a Circle of Friends who volunteer their services. Pacem has no paid staff. It has no "membership," hence no membership dues.

In February 1999, the New York State Board of Regents granted Pacem in Terris a provisional charter as a Museum, which after four years may become permanent.

HOW IS PACEM FINANCED?

One might well say: by a chain of miracles! For Pacem has neither fund-raisers nor PR, nor does it seek or receive corporation, or foundation, or state grants. Yet it has managed never to be in the red over the past three decades. It has been self-sustaining by tax-deductible unsolicited contributions and gifts, by subscriptions to its newsletter "The Shoestring," which has some two thousand subscribers, plus a very modest income from sale of the little visitor's guide: "The Story of Pacem in Terris." Pacem has no salaried staff.

Ezechiel: "I shall take out your heart of stone and give you a heart of flesh."
Steel, rock glass, 9 ft.

119

On a minimum budget, thanks to the commitment, the enthusiasm, and fidelity of all involved, its dedicated volunteers, the full-time efforts of Claske Berndes Franck as receptionist, organizer, correspondent, etc. and of Claske and Frederick's son Lukas in multiple ways, it has been possible to offer:

1. Free admission to the buildings, the Daito gallery, the "sculpture gardens," and grounds on weekends from May

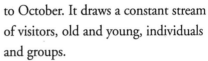

to October. It draws a constant stream of visitors, old and young, individuals and groups.

2. An annual series of classical chamber music concerts, since 1966, by professional artists of standing attracted by the ambience, the exceptional acoustics of the old mill with its high wooden roof as soundbox, and by the warm appreciation of dedicated music lovers. The concerts draw full-house audiences as a rule. The suggested donation has been kept minimal. There are a hundred simple seats available.

3. The ongoing creation and care of a circular, organic garden (vegetables, flowers, herbs), the "Resurgence Garden" as an ecological, horticultural learning experience and a delight for the eye.

4. The two "sculpture gardens," which house some seventy steel, wood, and stone icons.

5. Plays and poetry readings of cultural significance.

In short:

Chambermusic at Pacem in Terris

All programs presented by Pacem are selected to fit its contemplative character. They do not aspire to offer "en-

121

tertainment," but cultural and spiritual enhancement, enrichment, openness.

Pacem has nothing to sell, least of all any ideology. It is not connected, either directly or indirectly, to any political, religious, or ideological organization or movement. Someone had called Pacem "a Poor Man's Folly." I said: "Perhaps it is, although we are neither poor nor rich. Still, if it were a rich man's folly there would surely be admission charges, uniformed parking attendants, a gift shop, a restaurant." Pacem has none of these.

As a "not-for-profit" – perhaps the most "not-for-profit" in the country – it has been enormously profitable: innumerable letters of appreciation, friendship, and gratitude, and visitors' written remarks are proof of it.

THE FUTURE OF PACEM IN TERRIS

Our son, Lukas van Witsen Franck, co-president of Pacem in Terris, is fully committed to continue our life work. He is as devoted to Pacem as he is to his work with the blind, as part of the faculty of The Seeing Eye Foundation, Morristown, New Jersey, since 1983. He will act as curator for the full collection of works of art, sculptures, paintings, and drawings that we leave testamentally to Pacem in Terris and that we can trust Lukas to keep intact for future generations. Our will provides funding of Pacem in Terris for the foreseeable future.

Once asked, tactfully, about "the ulterior motive" hidden behind it, I explained that Pacem's ulterior motive is to prove that you can still do what you believe in without an ulterior motive. For us it is a thirty-five-year-long learning experience, discovering the human in humans, regardless of all that divides us: gender, color, creed, social position,

The Meaning of Life
Is to See! *(Hui Neng)*
Steel, 6 x 6 feet

123

age. Quite often people come with their children and tell us they visited Pacem with their parents as kids and now wanted to show it to their own children.

At this point, today's mail came. In it was this note, forwarded by Connie Carlough, one of Pacem's friends from the very beginning:

Fairlawn, August 5, 1998
Dear Ms. Carlough:
It's been many years since you taught me (1972) and my husband (1968) at Fairlawn High School. I want to let you know that it had far reaching effects.... More than twenty five years ago you took us on a "class trip" to Pacem in Terris: that very special place. My husband and I have returned to it ever since!

Each year we make it a point to introduce Pacem in Terrris to a few more special people who can appreciate its beauty and its stillness. To know that there is a place like this – a place to go and simply contemplate – fills me with peace. And so I wanted to say thank you for this special gift. I think of you at every visit.

Very truly yours,
Sharon and Ira

Left: Alpha and Omega:
The dam in winter

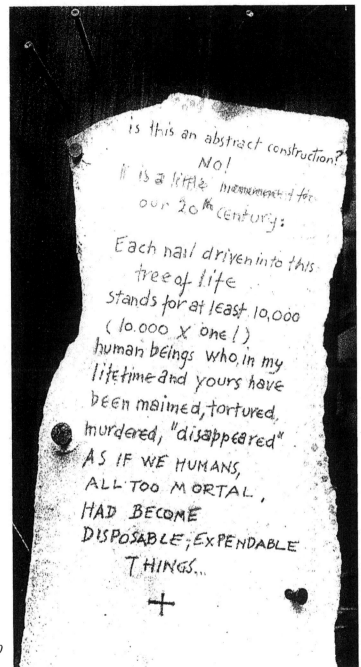

Tree of Nails:
7' high, about 1000 nails.

Colophon
Limited signed edition of 100 casebound copies.
Paperback first edition of 2,000 copies.
Design: Martin Moskof
Typesetting: Graphic Communications & Product Design, in Adobe Garamond. Designed by
Claude Garamond, a French type designer and
founder; c. 1480-1561. One of the first punch
cutters to work independently of printers. Perfected design of roman type and used it to replace the Gothic then commonly used.
Printing by Photo Comp Press, New York, N.Y.